W9-AAH-770

UNITED STATES

ARMY

by Jack David

Library of Congress
David, Jack, 1968–
 United States Army / by Jack David.
   p. cm. — (Torque: Armed Forces)
 Includes bibliographical references and index.
 ISBN-13: 978-1-60014-162-1 (hbk. : alk. paper)
 ISBN-10: 1-60014-162-5 (hbk. : alk. paper)
 1. United States. Army—Juvenile literature. I. Title.
 UA25.D28 2008
 355.00973–dc22   2007042407

CONTENTS

★ ★ ★

★ ★ ★

Chapter One

WHAT IS THE UNITED STATES ARMY?

Huge tanks rumble across the battlefield. The sound of gunfire fills the air. U.S. Army troops are in a tough ground battle. They have the training and equipment for exactly this kind of situation.

Infantry

The U.S. Army was established in 1775. General George Washington took command of the army and led it to victory over Great Britain in the Revolutionary War.

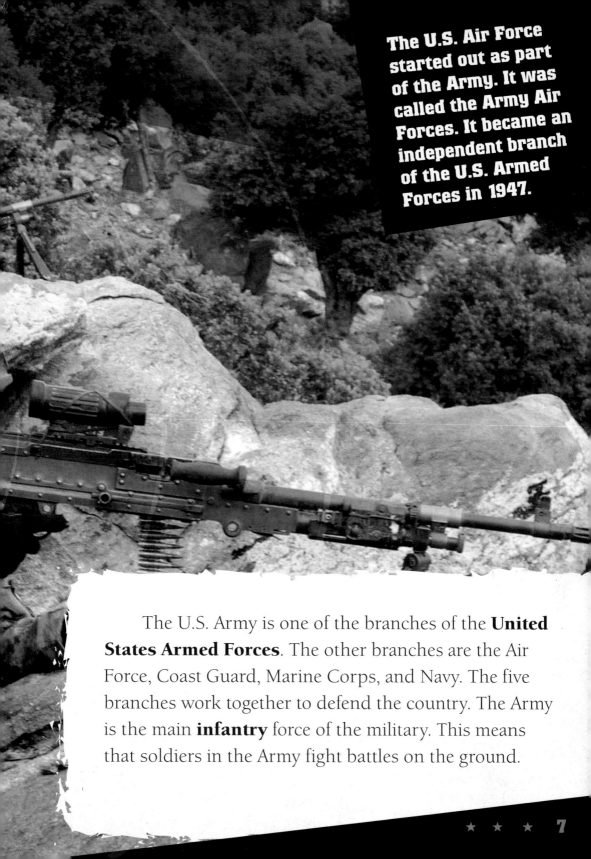

The U.S. Air Force started out as part of the Army. It was called the Army Air Forces. It became an independent branch of the U.S. Armed Forces in 1947.

The U.S. Army is one of the branches of the **United States Armed Forces**. The other branches are the Air Force, Coast Guard, Marine Corps, and Navy. The five branches work together to defend the country. The Army is the main **infantry** force of the military. This means that soldiers in the Army fight battles on the ground.

Chapter Two

VEHICLES, WEAPONS, AND TOOLS OF THE ARMY

M1 Abrams tank

The Army needs vehicles to accomplish its **missions**. Big tanks are covered with metal **armor**. Tanks such as the M1 Abrams have huge, powerful **main guns**. Tough tracks cover their wheels. They can roll across any kind of **terrain**. **Humvees** are trucks with armor. They can help fight battles. They can also carry wounded soldiers from a battlefield.

Main gun

Missiles

Helicopters are also important for the Army. Helicopters transport troops and supplies to wherever they are needed. They also support ground troops in battle. The AH-64 Apache is the Army's best combat helicopter. It uses guns and **missiles** to clear the way for ground troops.

The Apache helicopter can reach speeds of more than 260 miles (416 kilometers) per hour!

M4 Carbine

Soldiers need weapons to fight battles. Automatic guns such as the M4 Carbine can fire bullets very quickly. **Grenades** are small explosives that soldiers can either launch with a grenade launcher or throw by hand. Rocket launchers can destroy enemy aircraft. Rockets can also be aimed at tanks on the ground.

Rocket launcher

Camouflage

Army members use many other tools as well. Radios help commanders give orders to their troops. Night-vision goggles (NVGs) allow soldiers to see in the dark. Gas masks protect them from chemical attacks. **Camouflage** uniforms help them hide in many kinds of environments.

Chapter Three

LIFE IN THE ARMY

Life in the Army is different for every member. Some members serve overseas. They may serve in wars or provide **peacekeeping** support. They are often in danger. Other members serve at bases in the United States. They must always be ready to protect the country.

Every Army soldier has an important role. Everyone has a **rank** that determines his or her level of responsibility. Most soldiers are **enlisted members.** They start their service in **basic training**. They learn about combat, do exercises, and practice using weapons. Next, they get specialized job training. Some join the infantry. Others become mechanics, weapons specialists, cooks, and military police.

Basic training

The Army is the largest branch of the U.S. Armed Forces. It has more than 400,000 enlisted members and 76,000 officers.

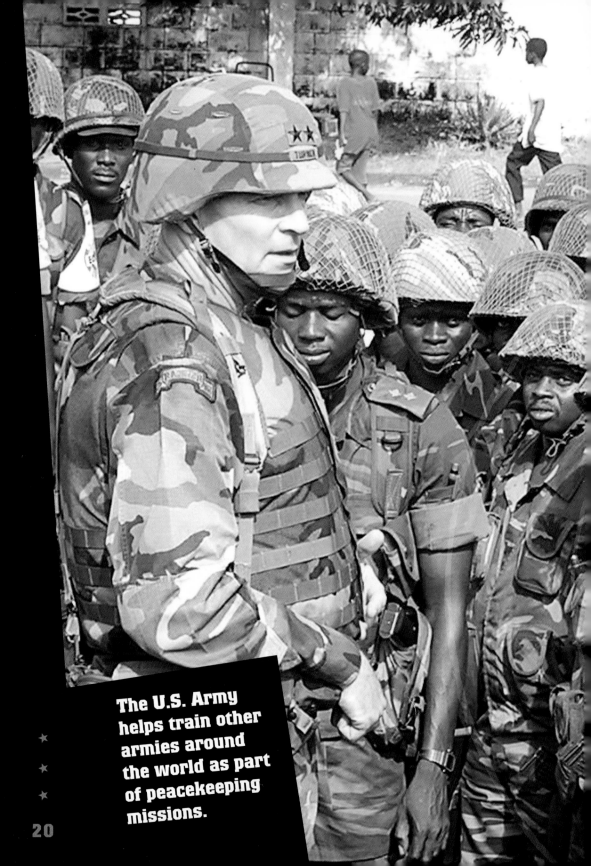

The U.S. Army
helps train other
armies around
the world as part
of peacekeeping
missions.

Officers are the leaders of the Army. They attend the Army's Officer Candidate School (OCS) at Fort Benning, Georgia. Officers learn combat strategies and how to give orders. The Army needs smart, effective leaders to accomplish its missions.

Officers

GLOSSARY

★ ★ ★

armor—protective plating

basic training—the course of drills, physical tests, and military training that new enlisted members of the U.S. Armed Forces go through

camouflage—made with patterns or colors that help someone blend into their surroundings

enlisted member—a person in the U.S. Armed Forces who ranks below an officer; all enlisted members are currently volunteers.

grenade—a small explosive that can be thrown or launched

humvee—a type of armored truck used by the Army

infantry—soldiers trained to fight on the ground

main gun—the large gun on top of a tank

missile—an explosive launched at targets on the ground or in the air

mission—a military task

officer—a member of the armed forces who ranks above enlisted members

peacekeeping—keeping the peace following the end of a conflict

rank—a specific position and level of responsibility in a group

terrain—the natural surface features of the land

United States Armed Forces—the five branches of the United States military; they are the Air Force, the Army, the Coast Guard, the Marine Corps, and the Navy.

TO LEARN MORE

★ ★ ★

AT THE LIBRARY

Bartlett, Richard. *United States Army*. Chicago, Ill.: Heinemann, 2003.

David, Jack. *Abrams Tanks*. Minneapolis, Minn.: Bellwether, 2008.

David, Jack. *Apache Helicopters*. Minneapolis, Minn.: Bellwether, 2008.

ON THE WEB

Learning more about the United States Army is as easy as 1, 2, 3.

1. Go to www.factsurfer.com

2. Enter "Army" into search box.

3. Click the "Surf" button and you will see a list of related web sites.

With factsurfer.com, finding more information is just a click away.